MW00965922

# SAMURAI!

## VALERIE BODDEN

JAPAN

CREATIVE EDUCATION · CREATIVE PAPERBACKS

Published by Creative Education and Creative Paperbacks • P.O. Box 227, Mankato, Minnesota 56002 • Creative Education and Creative Paperbacks are imprints of The Creative Company • www.thecreativecompany.us • Design by Rita Marshall • Production by Christine Vanderbeek • Printed in China • Photographs by Alamy (Tibor Bognar), Chronicle, Lebrecht Music and Arts Photo Library, Yannick luthy, Mary Evans Picture Library, Niday Picture Library, Photo Japan, Alexander Walker), Corbin (Alinari Archives, Asian Art & Archaeology Inc., Michael Maslan Historic Photographs), (DEA/G. DAGLI ORTI, John Stevenson), iStockphoto, Creative Commons Wikimedia (aluxum, Richmatts), (Library of Congress), Freevectormaps.com, Getty Images, Shutterstock (Jan Ceman, Nebojsa Kontic, Volodymyr Krasyuk, Stephen Marques), SuperStock (Iberfoto)

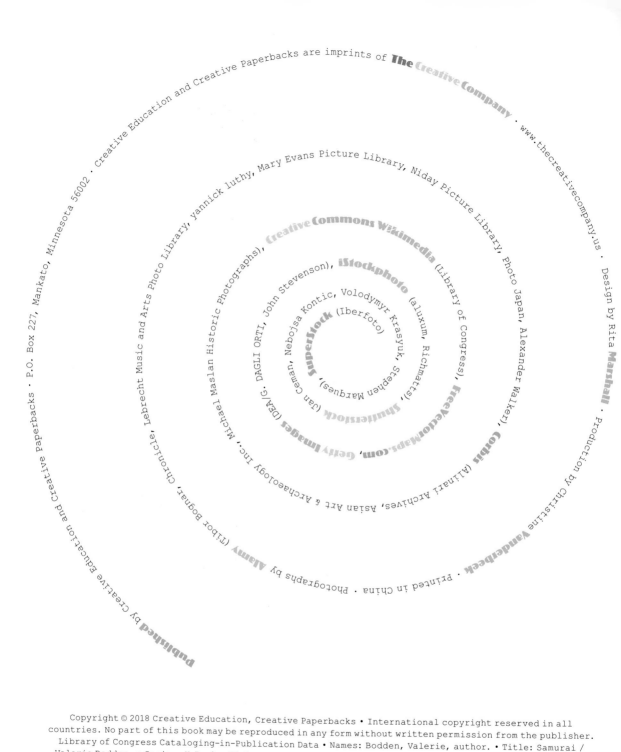

Copyright © 2018 Creative Education, Creative Paperbacks • International copyright reserved in all countries. No part of this book may be reproduced in any form without written permission from the publisher.

Library of Congress Cataloging-in-Publication Data • Names: Bodden, Valerie, author. • Title: Samurai / Valerie Bodden. • Series: X-Books: Fighters. • Includes bibliographical references and index. • Summary: A countdown of five of the most legendary samurai provides thrills as readers explore the lives, weapons, and battle tactics of these Japanese fighters. • IDENTIFIERS: LCCN 2016040390 / ISBN 978-1-60818-815-4 (HARDCOVER) / ISBN 978-1-62832-418-1 (PBK) / ISBN 978-1-56660-863-3 (EBOOK) • Subjects: LCSH: Samurai—Juvenile literature. • CLASSIFICATION: LCC DS827.S3 B64 2017 / DDC 952/.025—dc23 • CCSS: RI.3.1–8; RI.4.1–5, 7; RI.5.1–3, 8; RI.6.1–2, 4, 7; RH.6–8.3–8
First Edition HC 9 8 7 6 5 4 3 2 1 • First Edition PBK 9 8 7 6 5 4 3 2 1

# SAMURAI!

# JAPANESE HIERARCHY

**TOP**

| EMPEROR | ruler of Japan |
| DAIMYO | upper-class landowners |
| SAMURAI | noble fighters |
| FARMERS | land workers |
| CRAFTSMEN | makers of goods |
| MERCHANTS | shopkeepers |

**BOTTOM**

# XACTING FIGHTERS

For 700 years, samurai fought on the battlefields of Japan. These extreme fighters wielded swords and bows. Their goal was to win land for their master. They wanted to bring him honor.

## Samurai Basics

The word samurai is Japanese. It means "one who serves." Samurai warriors served wealthy landowners. These landowners were called daimyo. Each daimyo ruled over an area of land. The samurai served in the daimyo's army. They guarded his land. They fought to win new lands for their daimyo, too.

Samurai first fought in the 900s. They were part-time fighters. When they weren't fighting, they farmed the land. Later, the daimyo needed full-time armies. So they paid the samurai. They gave them homes, too. A samurai's only job was to be a soldier.

# IN ISOLATION

An island nation, Japan did not have much contact
with the rest of the world until the 1800s.

Japan

## THE UNITED STATES SENT SHIPS

to Japan in 1854. Many samurai were angry

that the government allowed Americans

to enter the country. Civil war broke out.

## DAIMYO CASTLES

Daimyo lived in castles surrounded by strong walls. Some samurai lived in the castle, too. Others lived in nearby buildings called barracks.

## DAIMYO CASTLES WERE BUILT

on hills or mountains. A fort with strong walls surrounded the castle. Samurai barracks were inside the walls. Samurai were always ready for a fight.

## SOME DAIMYO GAVE SAMURAI

pieces of land. The samurai ruled over the workers and farmers on that land.

Girls from samurai families did not train with weapons. But they did have martial arts training. They knew how to defend their homes if the men were away.

SAMURAI FAMILIES

In Japan, only samurai could carry weapons. At first, anyone could become a samurai. Later, the role of samurai was passed down from father to son. Anyone whose father was not a samurai could not become one. Samurai usually married women from other samurai families.

Samurai did not question their master.

SAMURAI WERE LOYAL

## SAMURAI BASICS FACT

When not fighting, some samurai wrote **calligraphy** or played the **lute**.

# 5

Xtreme Samurai #5

**Miyamoto Musashi** studied martial arts when he was a child. At the age of 13, he killed a samurai in a one-on-one fight. In 1600, Musashi's master was defeated in battle. He became a ronin, or a masterless samurai. Musashi traveled across Japan fighting **duels**. By the time he was 29, he had won more than 60 fights. He had not lost any. Musashi was also a painter and a writer.

The best samurai became famous.

People told stories about their successes.

Artists made paintings of them.

# Life as a Samurai

Boys from samurai families started training around the age of seven. They studied under experienced samurai. Students and teachers formed a strong bond.

Young samurai studied reading and poetry. They also learned fighting skills. Young warriors practiced martial arts. They fought each other with wooden swords. Around the age of 15, they were considered samurai.

Samurai followed a special code called bushido. Bushido means "way of the warrior." The code showed how a samurai should behave.

Above all, a samurai had to be loyal to his master. Bushido also stressed bravery and honesty. Much of bushido had to do with death. Samurai were supposed to think about death often. That way, they would be ready to die in battle.

Japan is ruled by an emperor

**900s**

Warring Period begins

**1400s**

First samurai fight | Daimyo gain power | Fights among daimyo | Gun usage begins

Shogun overpowers emperor

**1185**

**1540s**

Warring Period ends

**1600s**

Emperor returns to power

**1868**

Peace in Japan | New law passed | Civil war breaks out | Samurai system ends

Samurai duels are outlawed

**1650**

**1871**

## LIFE AS A SAMURAI FACT

A samurai who was defeated in battle might kill himself.

This was called seppuku.

## TOP FIVE XTREME SAMURAI

Xtreme Samurai #4

**Kusunoki Masashige** fought for Japan's emperor in the 1300s. When the emperor's castle was overrun, Masashige led sneak attacks. He beat the enemy. Later, the emperor was attacked again. Masashige wanted to use sneak attacks again. But the emperor ordered him to fight on the battlefield. Masashige obeyed and was defeated. Today, he is seen as a model of loyalty for obeying his master.

# XCESSIVE BATTLE

Samurai rode into battle wearing layers of armor. The most famous samurai weapon was the sword. But samurai used other weapons as well.

Many samurai were skilled archers.

ARCHERS SHOT ARROWS

## SAMURAI WEAPONS FACT

Samurai did not use shields.

They used their katana to block the enemy's sword.

Samurai armor was often colorful. It might be red, gold, or purple. It could have fancy designs.

# Samurai Weapons

For battle, a samurai put on armor that covered most of his body. Some samurai wore a large, solid plate on top. This plate was made of metal or leather. Others wore armor made up of many smaller plates tied together. A samurai's legs were covered with a skirt of armor. A metal helmet protected the samurai's head.

Most samurai carried two swords. The first was a long, curved sword. It was called a katana. A samurai needed two hands to swing it. Samurai also carried a shorter sword, or dagger. This could be used for up-close fighting. Many samurai also wielded spears.

Early samurai used bows and arrows, too. In 1542, explorers from Portugal came to Japan. The samurai were amazed by their guns. Soon, the Japanese were making their own guns. They called the guns teppo.

# XPLOSIVE TACTICS

The daimyo was the head of the samurai army. He made decisions about who to fight. He came up with the battle plan, too.

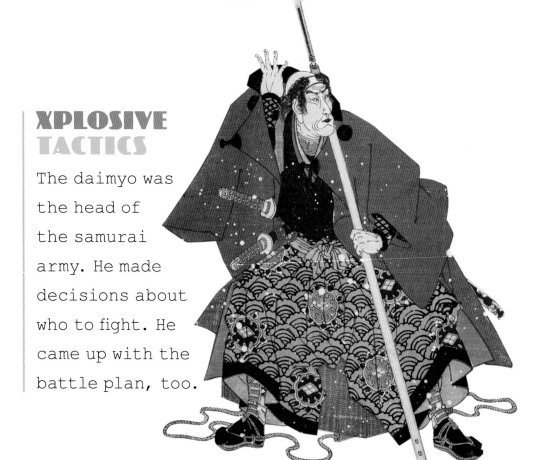

## XPLOSIVE TACTICS FACT

Sometimes samurai surrounded an enemy's fort.
They did not let any food or water in.

Some of the lower-ranking samurai carried flags. The flags were used to communicate on the battlefield.

Two samurai armies faced each other across a battlefield. Each could have 50,000 fighters. The daimyo set up behind his army. From there, he sent orders to the samurai. The daimyo's relatives served as officers. They carried the daimyo's orders to the samurai at the front.

Sometimes the samurai tried to trick their enemies. They might pretend to retreat. The enemy would follow them. Then, other samurai who were hiding attacked.

Xtreme Samurai #3

**The 47 Ronin** In 1701, a daimyo named Lord Asano visited the palace of the Japanese ruler. There, another daimyo named Lord Kira insulted him. So Asano pulled out his sword. It was illegal for anyone to draw a sword in the palace. Asano was forced to kill himself. His samurai became ronin, or masterless. Two years later, 47 of the ronin killed Kira. Then they killed themselves.

# XTENSIVE LEGACY

By the 1600s, Japan was at peace. Samurai didn't have much to do. The government had to outlaw dueling in 1650 to keep bored samurai from killing one another.

## Samurai Legacy

In 1871, the Japanese emperor ended the samurai system. Many samurai led rebellions against him. But they were not successful. Afterward, some samurai joined Japan's new army. Others took jobs in Japanese government and business.

The samurai influence can still be felt today. Many Japanese businesses follow the bushido code. People around the world practice the samurai's discipline of martial arts.

Samurai remain popular in books and movies, too. The Jedi knights of the *Star Wars* movies are modeled after samurai. The samurai era may be over. But the spirit of these extreme fighters lives on.

Samurai spent time in quiet thought.

They tried to control their fears.

They learned to think quickly.

Meditation helped samurai focus their minds.

During World War II, many Japanese soldiers followed the bushido code. They flew their planes into enemy ships. They knew they would die in the attacks. But they were following in the footsteps of traditional samurai. Sometimes samurai killed themselves if they broke the bushido code. Most samurai committed seppuku by slicing their stomach open.

## XTENSIVE LEGACY FACT

Many people still practice kendo,

a samurai martial art using bamboo swords.

Xtreme Samurai #2

**Oda Nobunaga** was a daimyo. He was one of the first to give his samurai guns. In 1560, his 3,000 men defeated an army of 25,000. Then Nobunaga marched through the country. He conquered many lands. Nobunaga could be cruel. He once set fire to a fortress. Everyone inside was killed. In 1582, one of Nobunaga's samurai attacked him. Nobunaga was injured. He knew he couldn't escape. So he killed himself.

Tomoe Gozen was a female samurai.
She was skilled with a spear and bow and arrow.

Samurai armor could stop arrows. One samurai was hit by 20 arrows before he died.

Samurai wives wore long hairpins. They could use the hairpins as weapons.

A samurai who had been insulted was allowed to kill the person who insulted him.

Samurai shaved the front part of their hair. They pulled the rest into a topknot.

When they weren't in battle, samurai wore long, flowing robes called kimonos.

Some samurai wore metal face masks with scary expressions.

Sword makers prayed and bathed before making a sword. They wore all white.

The best samurai archer could hit a target more than 8,000 times in 24 hours.

Stirrups allowed samurai to stand while riding. This made it easier to fire their bows.

Samurai inside a surrounded fort poured boiling water over the walls.

Samurai often cut off the heads of their dead enemies.

Sometimes samurai killed everyone in a defeated village.

If a samurai bumped

nto the sword of another samurai, the two fought on the spot.

Xtreme Samurai #1

**Saigo Takamori** was one of the last samurai. He opened a school for military training. He soon had 20,000 students. But Takamori was unhappy with the changes the government was making. In January 1877, he led a rebellion against the emperor. He suffered many defeats. Then he was seriously wounded. He asked one of his warriors to cut off his head.

## GLOSSARY

**calligraphy** — decorative handwriting

**duels** — fights between two people, usually with weapons

**lute** — a stringed instrument similar to a guitar

**martial arts** — systems of fighting styles designed for combat or self-defense

## RESOURCES

Miller, David. *Samurai Warriors*. New York: Thomas Dunne, 2000.

Sinclaire, Clive. *Samurai: The Weapons and Spirit of the Japanese Warrior*. Guilford, Conn.: Lyons Press, 2001.

Turnbull, Stephen. *Samurai: The Story of Japan's Great Warriors*. New York: PRC, 2004.

———. *Samurai: The World of the Warrior*. New York: Osprey, 2003.

## INDEX

A samurai never went anywhere unarmed—even indoors.